WE THE PEOPLE

AMERICAN PATRIOT
BENJAMIN FRANKLIN

by Michael Burgan

Content Adviser: Richard Bell,
Department of History,
University of Maryland

Reading Adviser: Alexa L. Sandmann, Ed.D.,
Professor of Literacy, College and Graduate School
of Education, Health, and Human Services,
Kent State University

Compass Point Books ✦ Minneapolis, Minnesota

Compass Point Books
151 Good Counsel Drive
P.O. Box 669
Mankato, MN 56002-0669

 This book was manufactured with paper containing at least 10 percent post-consumer waste.

On the cover: Benjamin Franklin (left), John Adams, and Thomas Jefferson met to review a draft of the Declaration of Independence in 1776.

Photographs ©: Library of Congress, cover, 16, 33, 36; The Bridgeman Art Library/Getty Images, 4; Stock Montage/Getty Images, 5; Bettmann/Corbis, 6, 18, 41; North Wind Picture Archives, 8, 11, 35; The Granger Collection, New York, 10, 13, 14, 27, 28; Herbert Orth/Time Life Pictures/Getty Images, 15; Mary Evans Picture Library, 19; Private Collection/Look and Learn/The Bridgeman Art Library, 20; Atwater Kent Museum of Philadelphia/The Bridgeman Art Library, 22; Bibliotheque Nationale, Paris, France/Lauros/Giraudon/The Bridgeman Art Library, 25; Line of Battle Enterprise, 30; Private Collection/The Bridgeman Art Library, 31, 39; Architect of the Capitol, 40.

Editor: Mari Bolte
Page Production: Bobbie Nuytten
Photo Researcher: Svetlana Zhurkin
Cartographer: XNR Productions, Inc.
Library Consultant: Kathleen Baxter

Art Director: LuAnn Ascheman-Adams
Creative Director: Joe Ewest
Editorial Director: Nick Healy
Managing Editor: Catherine Neitge

Library of Congress Cataloging-in-Publication Data
Burgan, Michael.
  American patriot : Benjamin Franklin / by Michael Burgan.
     p. cm. — (We the People)
  Includes index.
  ISBN 978-0-7565-4119-4 (library binding)
  1. Franklin, Benjamin 1706–1790—Juvenile literature. 2. Statesmen—United States—Biography—Juvenile literature. 3. Inventors—United States—Biography—Juvenile literature. 4. Scientists—United States—Biography—Juvenile literature. 5. Printers—United States—Biography—Juvenile literature. I. Title.
  E302.6.F8B8935 2009
  973.3092—dc22   2008037632

Visit Compass Point Books on the Internet at *www.compasspointbooks.com* or e-mail your request to *custserv@compasspointbooks.com*

Table of Contents

Talented Patriot

*I*n London's beautiful Westminster Abbey, King George III of Great Britain and his new wife, Charlotte, received their crowns in September 1761. Also at the church that day was a loyal English subject from America— Benjamin Franklin. Lawmakers in the American colony of Pennsylvania had asked Franklin to represent them in Great Britain. In Philadelphia, the capital of the colony, he was respected for

King George III (1738–1820) is the longest reigning male monarch in British history.

his intelligence and public service. Franklin was also an honored scientist and inventor. The British enjoyed having him in London, and he thought about staying there forever.

Within 15 years, his position had changed. Franklin made enemies in London. King George and his advisers wanted to strengthen British con-

Benjamin Franklin crossed the Atlantic Ocean eight times and visited 10 countries in his lifetime.

trol over the American colonies. Franklin eventually sided with Americans, called patriots, who resisted this effort. Franklin had once called himself the "mortal enemy of … unlimited power."

Over the years, he had seen that the British treated the colonies unfairly. In 1775, Franklin returned to America and joined the patriot cause.

When the time came to declare American independence

Franklin (left) is one of America's Founding Fathers.

from Great Britain, Franklin realized that he and the patriots were rebels in the eyes of King George. He said they had to "hang together, or assuredly we shall all hang separately." Franklin knew that if the colonies did not work together to win independence, their leaders would be punished for opposing the king.

During the Revolutionary War, Franklin sought help from France for the new United States. After the Americans won, he helped shape the Constitution, which created the U.S. government. Throughout his life, Franklin tried to be the best person he could be. Born poor, he became wealthy. Throughout his long life, he worked hard and used his talents to help others. His life is a model many Americans have tried to follow.

Learning a Trade

*B*oston was a small, lively seaport when Benjamin Franklin was born there on January 17, 1706. He was the youngest son in the large Franklin family of 17 children. His father, Josiah, made candles and soaps. Young Ben wanted to be

Benjamin was the 10th son and last child born to Josiah and Abiah Franklin.

a sailor, because he loved swimming and sailboats. His father, however, wanted him to be a minister, so he sent Ben to school. Ben did well in reading and writing. By age 10, he had left school to work in his father's shop.

Ben used the money his father paid him to buy his favorite things. As Franklin later wrote, "… all the little money that came into my hands was ever laid out in [spent on] books." When he was 12, Ben became an apprentice printer. His older brother James ran a printing shop in Boston. There, Ben helped run the shop and learned the business. In return, James gave Ben room and board. The shop printed papers, pamphlets, and books, so Ben had plenty to read.

In 1721, James Franklin began publishing the *New-England Courant*, the third newspaper ever in the American colonies. At 16, Ben wrote articles for the paper. For a time he printed it as well, after his brother was sent to jail for writing several articles that

THE
New-England Courant.

From MONDAY February 4. to MONDAY February 11. 172¾.

Benjamin often used pseudonyms (fake names) when writing his articles. Fifteen of his letters were published in the New-England Courant under his first pseudonym, Silence Dogood.

upset local officials in Boston.

Ben enjoyed writing and publishing the paper, but he didn't get along with his brother. In 1723, the younger Franklin left and headed for New York. He tried to get a job with a printer there. The printer did not have a job for Franklin but thought his son in Philadelphia might have work. The son, Andrew Bradford, was also a printer. After a long, tiring trip by boat and on foot, Franklin finally reached Philadelphia. Bradford did not have work for him, but a printer named Samuel Keimer did.

Pennsylvania's governor, William Keith, read a letter that Franklin wrote while Franklin was working for Keimer. Keith visited Keimer's shop and, as Franklin later recorded, "made me many compliments." The governor wanted to help Franklin set up his own printing shop. In November 1724, he sent Franklin to London with the promise that Keith would pay for equipment.

Governor Keith offered to write introduction letters and letters of credit, which would allow Franklin to meet other printers and purchase printing materials in London.

3 Hard Times and Good Times

*I*n the 18th century, ships provided the only link between North America and Great Britain. The trip took seven weeks. When Ben Franklin arrived in London, he learned that Governor Keith had not sent the letters of credit he had promised Franklin. These letters would have allowed Franklin to purchase printing equipment. With no money of his own, Franklin had to find a job. He spent almost two years in London working as a printer.

Franklin returned to Philadelphia in October 1726 at the age of 20. Years of hard work had turned him into an excellent printer. Within three years, he owned his own shop and a popular newspaper, the *Pennsylvania Gazette*. He also became the official printer for the government of Pennsylvania.

By this time, Franklin had formed a club called the Junto. Its members wrote essays and discussed them and other things

The ship Franklin took to England sailed once a year between Philadelphia and London. Franklin had to wait nearly six months for his departure.

they read. Franklin's goal was to help himself and other trades-

men become educated, well-informed citizens.

Franklin was busy in his private life as well. Some time

around 1730, Franklin fathered a son, William. He did not

marry the boy's mother, but he raised William on his own.

Deborah Read (1708–1774)

Soon, though, he had help. In September 1730, he married Deborah Read, a woman he had met soon after he'd first arrived in Philadelphia in 1723. With his family and his thriving business, Franklin was becoming a respected citizen of Philadelphia. His success grew when he began publishing *Poor Richard's Almanack* in 1732. His yearly almanac, and others like it, printed yearly weather forecasts and predictions. Writing under the name Richard Saunders, he included short, sometimes funny, sayings.

"Fish and visitors," he wrote, "smell after three days." Franklin was known throughout his life for his sense of humor.

Franklin always seemed to have new projects. Shortly before he began his almanac, he helped create the first subscription library in North America. Members paid fees to buy books

Poor Richard's Almanack *sold an average of 10,000 copies a year.*

for the library and, in return, could borrow them when they wanted. In 1736, Franklin helped start Philadelphia's first fire company. Members volunteered to keep firefighting equipment available and to help put out fires. During the 1740s, Franklin also proposed starting a new school in Philadelphia—the University of Pennsylvania. His American Philosophical Society promoted research on a number of topics, especially science.

By 1770, Franklin's library held more than 2,000 books, with subjects ranging from religion, education, and philosophy to politics and business.

4 Inventor and Scientist

Ben Franklin had a deep interest in the natural world. He also enjoyed thinking of new ways to make life easier or better. Now with his business a success, he had the money to stop working in his shop and focus on science and inventions. Starting in the 1740s, he invented several items.

In 1742, Franklin built a fireplace that created more heat with less wood than other fireplaces at the time. The Franklin stove became popular in America and Britain. He also created bifocals—eyeglasses with the top half of the lenses designed to help see distances and the bottom half to help with reading. Other inventions included a candle that lasted longer and burned brighter than others and improvements to the printing press.

During Franklin's lifetime, many scientists were experimenting with electricity. Franklin became interested in it as well.

Franklin often wrote papers explaining how his inventions worked so other people could use them.

He learned how to create electrical sparks and send electricity over wires. In one experiment, he killed a turkey with an electrical jolt. Not all the experiments went well. In 1750, while trying to kill another turkey, Franklin gave himself a huge electrical shock. He wrote, "The Company present … Say that the flash was very great and the crack as loud as a Pistol." Franklin, however, was too stunned by the shock to notice.

Franklin's work with electricity led to one of his greatest

inventions—the lightning rod. Franklin saw that a metal rod placed on a building would draw lightning toward it and away from the building. A wire would then direct the electricity into the ground. Franklin was also the first person to suggest that lightning and electricity were the same

Franklin had his own physics lab in Philadelphia.

thing. In 1752, two Frenchmen tested his ideas, using a metal rod to draw lightning from a storm cloud. Franklin used a kite and a key to prove it as well. The electricity in the lightning traveled down the kite string and into the key. Franklin then drew

Franklin's son William helped devise the kite and key experiment.

sparks from the electrified key. Franklin won honors in both

America and Europe for his achievements. Many people began to

call him Dr. Franklin, and he was even awarded honorary doctor-

ates from Oxford and St. Andrews universities.

5 Public Servant

*B*en Franklin also found time for politics and public affairs. During the 18th century, France and Great Britain often battled each other for control of North American land. In 1747, Franklin proposed that Pennsylvania create a militia to defend against French or Indian attacks. The next year, he was elected to his first public office, serving on Philadelphia's Common Council. This council included the mayor and made laws for the city. For a time, Franklin also served as a judge, even though he had no formal training as a lawyer. And in 1751, he was elected to the Pennsylvania Assembly.

Two years later, Franklin took on a new government job, becoming one of two men in charge of the mail for all of the American colonies. During Franklin's time, mail delivery, especially mail delivered between Great Britain and the colonies, was unreliable. It might take two weeks for a single letter to travel the 110 miles (176 kilometers) between Philadelphia and New York. Franklin would greatly improve postal service in the colonies. He traveled across America and inspected the postal system to make sure it ran smoothly.

As the postmaster of Philadelphia, Franklin decreased by half the length of time for mail delivery between major cities in the colonies.

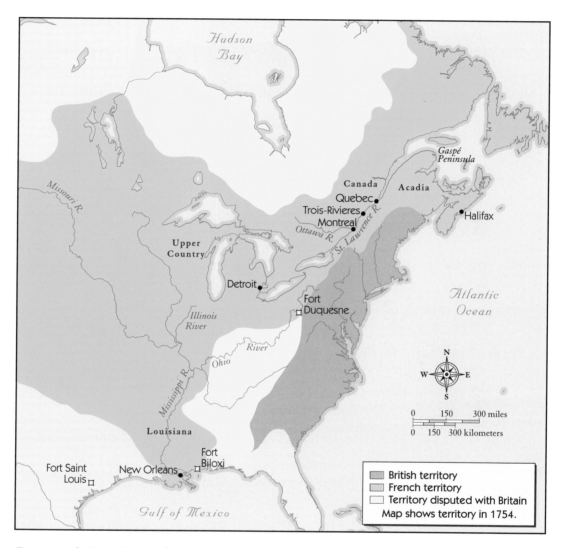

On the map:

Hudson Bay

Gaspé Peninsula

Canada

Quebec

Acadia

Trois-Rivieres

Montreal

Ottawa R.

St. Lawrence R.

Halifax

Upper Country

Detroit

Fort Duquesne

Atlantic Ocean

Illinois River

Ohio River

Missouri R.

Mississippi R.

Louisiana

Fort Biloxi

Fort Saint Louis

New Orleans

Gulf of Mexico

N W E S

0   150   300 miles
0   150   300 kilometers

British territory
French territory
Territory disputed with Britain
Map shows territory in 1754.

France and Great Britain fought for control of the colonies during the French and Indian War.

The next year, he traveled again, but on a different mission. What would later be known as the French and Indian War was about to break out between the French and the British in the colonies. Franklin went to Albany, New York, to meet with other colonial leaders. He proposed that the colonies unite to defend themselves. The idea was rejected because the colonies liked having their own governments.

As the French and Indian War began, Franklin helped the British by gathering food and supplies. Late in 1755, he was made an officer of the Pennsylvania militia and led troops that built small forts to defend the Pennsylvania frontier.

The war lasted until 1763, but Franklin was in Britain for most of it. In 1757, the Pennsylvania Assembly had asked him to go to London. The lawmakers were battling the governor over taxes, and they hoped Franklin could persuade British officials to help them. In 1757, he traveled to Britain with his son William and two servants, starting an important new part of his life.

Trouble in the Colonies

Ben Franklin spent five years in Britain. He persuaded the British government to allow the Assembly to tax lands belonging to the Penn family, which had founded Pennsylvania and owned a large portion of the colony. The tax money they would be forced to pay would finance the war.

When Franklin returned to America in 1762, fighting between France and Britain was over. The war officially ended in 1763, with

Taxes would eventually be placed on everyday items such as sugar, tea, and paper.

the British taking control of almost all of France's former lands east of the Mississippi River.

In the fall of 1764, Franklin returned to London to represent Pennsylvania again. By the next year, trouble was stirring between Britain and the colonies. Winning the French and Indian War had been expensive, and Britain knew that its new territories would cost even more. The British believed the Americans should help pay these costs through higher taxes. The Americans, however, did not want to pay more than they already did.

The British collected new taxes in 1764, sparking protests in the colonies. The Americans reacted even more violently the next year when the British Parliament passed the Stamp Act. This law placed a tax on papers and documents used in the colonies. Before, Parliament only taxed imported or exported items—never goods used within the colonies. The Americans said the new tax was unfair. Plus they were denied their rights as British citizens to

Under the Stamp Act, every piece of printed paper was taxed. This included legal documents, newspapers, pamphlets, and even playing cards.

have representatives in Parliament to defend their interests.

At first, Franklin supported the right of Parliament to collect

the taxes. He wrote a friend that loyalty to the king and the British

government "will always be the wisest Course for you and I to take."

Colonists protested in the streets after Parliament passed the Stamp Act.

But across the colonies, patriots attacked the men chosen to collect the new tax. Some also damaged the homes of a few British officials. When Franklin heard about the violence, he realized how angry many Americans were. He hoped to find a peaceful end to the problem.

By February 1766, many colonists refused to buy British goods. Franklin spoke to Parliament, asking them to repeal the

Stamp Act. He pointed out how hard the new tax was on many Americans. He suggested that trying to force the Americans to pay could lead to war. By then, British merchants were also calling for a repeal of the law. They were losing money because the colonists were not buying their goods. Parliament agreed to repeal the tax, but it said it had the right to collect new taxes in the future.

In 1767, the British did place new taxes on the colonies. This led to more protests, especially in Boston. Afraid of rioting, the British government sent more than 4,000 troops to the city. In 1770, violence broke out between them and local men. The British soldiers killed five residents in what would be known as the Boston Massacre. Three years later, some patriots protested a tax on tea. They threw more than 300 crates of tea into the harbor, an event later called the Boston Tea Party.

By that time, Franklin was representing Massachusetts and two other colonies besides Pennsylvania. He was the most

Hostility between the colonists and British soldiers led to the Boston Massacre.

famous American in London—and perhaps the most disliked.

In 1774, he damaged the reputation of Thomas Hutchinson, the

governor of Massachusetts, by releasing letters that the gover-

nor had written. The letters suggested that the governor wanted

British troops to deny the colonists their rights. Franklin was

summoned to London where he was humiliated and stripped

of his postmaster general title. This, along with the death of his

beloved wife, convinced Franklin to return home.

After the Boston Tea Party, King George III closed the harbor. This prevented the colonies from receiving goods from any country except Great Britain.

The British continued to take tighter control of Massachusetts. Local governments could not meet, ships could not leave or enter Boston Harbor, and a British general served as governor. Franklin still hoped the colonies and the British could settle their differences. He told a friend, "Quarrelling can be ... ruin to both." Franklin knew he could no longer help the colonies, and he sailed for home in March 1775.

7 War and Independence

When Ben Franklin reached Philadelphia in May, the colonies and Britain were at war. The month before, the two sides had clashed outside Boston at Lexington and Concord. This was the beginning of the war. Thousands of patriots across New England streamed into the Boston area to join the fight. Meanwhile, patriot leaders met and formed the Second Continental Congress. Franklin soon joined them, and the Congress debated what to do next.

Franklin had wanted to remain loyal to Britain. Now, though, he realized the Americans had to become independent if they wanted to keep their legal rights. Congress, however, did not consider this idea until June 1776. Franklin was one of five men chosen to write a declaration of independence. Thomas Jefferson wrote the document, while Franklin and others offered advice.

Benjamin Franklin (left), John Adams, and Thomas Jefferson met often to discuss the future of the colonies.

On July 2, the members of the Second Continental Congress voted for independence. Two days later, they approved the final version of Jefferson's declaration. The American colonies were on their way to becoming the United States of America.

Franklin still hoped to avoid a long war. In September 1776, he and two other members of Congress met with a British general in New York. The British, however, would not accept American independence. Soon after, Franklin left for France as an American diplomat. He hoped to win French aid for the war. Franklin, now 70 years old, was idolized in France for his scientific work. The French also liked his simple way of dressing and his way with words. They copied the fur hat he wore, and paintings and sculptures of him appeared across Paris, the French capital.

Within a few months of Franklin's arrival, the French government gave the Americans money and eventually agreed to send troops to America. Early in 1778, Franklin helped write treaties that brought even more French aid.

In 1781, French troops and ships played a large role in an important American victory. In October, the French and Americans defeated the British at Yorktown, Virginia. That loss convinced many British leaders they should end the war.

The British defeat at Yorktown became official on October 19, 1781.

As a result, America acquired new lands west of the 13 states—and its independence. The treaty between Britain and America, known as the Treaty of Paris, was signed in 1783, and Franklin finally returned home two years later.

Last Years

*B*en Franklin returned to Philadelphia in September 1785 and received a hero's welcome. Church bells rang, people cheered, and greeters carried him down the street. His wife,

After returning home, Franklin concentrated his attention on his family, the government, and abolishing slavery.

Deborah, had died in 1774, so Franklin lived with his daughter,
Sarah, and her family. He built a library in their house to hold
his massive book collection and scientific instruments. He hoped
to retire and to spend more time with his grandchildren. However,
problems in the new United States soon drew him back into
government affairs.

The first government of the country was outlined in a document called the Articles of Confederation. Under the articles,
the national government was weak. The 13 states sometimes
acted like mini-nations and ignored the national government.
Congress did not have the power to force the states to pay taxes.
Without taxes, the country could not pay debts or build a military.

By 1787, some U.S. leaders believed the United States
needed to improve the Articles of Confederation. The national
government needed more power. In May, every state except
Rhode Island sent representatives to a meeting in Philadelphia.

Pennsylvania asked Franklin to serve as one of its representatives. In his early 80s, he was the oldest member.

Not all the delegates agreed on how to change the Articles of Confederation. To settle one issue, Franklin promoted a compromise suggested by a delegate from Connecticut. The states couldn't agree on how many representatives each of them should have in Congress. Franklin suggested the Congress should have two parts. In one, called the House of Representatives, the population of a state would decide the number of its members. In the Senate, however, each state would have two representatives, called senators. The delegates accepted this plan, which was called the Great Compromise.

By September, the delegates had created a new national government for the United States. They wrote a document called the Constitution, which outlined the form of the new government and how it would work. The Philadelphia meeting was later called the Constitutional Convention.

When it came time to sign the document, Franklin had some words for the delegates. Too sick to speak himself, he had a friend give his speech for him. He said that there were parts of the Constitution that he did not agree with, but that he also did not disagree with them. He supported it because "I expect no better, and because I am not sure that it is not the best."

The Constitution was then given to the states, so they could decide whether

The Constitutional Convention met five days a week. Franklin never missed a session.

Franklin was the only person to sign the three documents key to American freedom: the Declaration of Independence, the Treaty of Paris, and the U.S. Constitution.

to accept it. The document was approved, and in March 1789,

the new U.S. Congress met for the first time.

By that time, Franklin was retired from public life. He

spent some time writing his autobiography, which he had started

working on in 1771. It was finally completed in 1788. However,

he soon became so sick he could not leave his bedroom. He

died on April 17, 1790, and was buried in Philadelphia next to

his wife, Deborah. Thousands of people came to his funeral. The

next year, President George Washington was one of many U.S.

leaders who attended a special service for Franklin. They came

to honor a man still remembered today for his writings, his say-

ings, and his actions.

Benjamin Franklin

helped create the

United States, and

today he remains one

of the greatest thinkers

and leaders the coun-

try has ever produced.

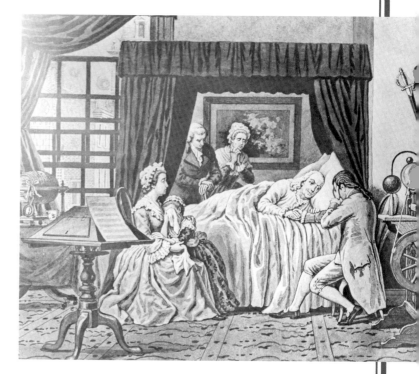

Benjamin Franklin was 84 years old when he died.
His funeral was attended by 20,000 people.

Glossary

apprentice—person who learns a job by living with and working for someone who already does that job

assembly—group of elected lawmakers

colony—territory settled by people from another country and controlled by that country

compromise—solutions that settle differences between people

delegates—people who represent a larger group of people at a meeting

diplomat—person who manages a country's affairs with other nations

frontier—largely unsettled border areas of a region

militia—group of citizens who have been organized to fight as a group but who are not professional soldiers

repeal—officially cancel an existing law

Second Continental Congress—group of American colonists who established laws and addressed problems with the British

subject—person who lives under the rule of a king or queen

subscription—arrangement to pay a fee and receive goods or services over time

Did You Know?

- Benjamin Franklin owned several slaves during most of his life. He eventually freed them and began speaking out against slavery. In 1787, he served as president of a Pennsylvania group that wanted to end slavery.

- One of Franklin's inventions was a musical instrument called the glass armonica. A wooden box contained glass cups of different sizes. The glasses spun within the box. A person made musical notes by putting a wet finger on the spinning glass. Although the armonica is rare today, some musicians still perform with it.

- During his travels back and forth across the Atlantic Ocean, Franklin learned about the Gulf Stream. These warm ocean waters form in the Gulf of Mexico and move toward northern Europe. Franklin was the first scientist to study the Gulf Stream. He measured its temperature and speed, as well as the speed of the winds near it.

- In his home, Franklin played tricks with electricity. One trick involved a piece of wire with smaller wires coming off it to serve as legs. When he ran an electrical current through the wire, it seemed to walk like an insect on its wire legs.

Important Dates

Timeline

1706	Born January 17 in Boston
1718	Begins serving as apprentice to his brother James
1723	Leaves Boston to begin new life in Philadelphia
1730	Marries Deborah Read
1732	Publishes first *Poor Richard's Almanack*
1752	Conducts experiment with kite to prove that lightning is made of electricity
1757	Moves to London to represent Pennsylvania Assembly in Great Britain
1775	Returns to Philadelphia and joins the Second Continental Congress
1776	Signs Declaration of Independence
1778	Helps win aid from France to help United States fight Great Britain
1787	Attends the Constitutional Convention in Philadelphia
1790	Dies April 17 in Philadelphia

Important People

William Franklin (1731–1813)

The older of Benjamin Franklin's two sons and the only one to reach adulthood, he served as the royal governor of colonial New Jersey; he opposed the American Revolution and in 1776 was arrested by patriots; he eventually settled in London

King George III (1738–1820)

King of England whose family traced its roots to Germany; he was the first king from the family born in Great Britain; his desire to raise taxes and increase control in the colonies led to the American Revolution; he suffered physical problems that affected his mental health, and spent the last years of his life outside of the public's view

Thomas Jefferson (1743–1826)

Third president of the United States, he served on the committee that wrote the Declaration of Independence and was the main author of that important document; he was also an inventor and created a new kind of plow and improved a device for writing two copies of a letter at once

William Keith (1669–1749)

The son of a noble Scottish family, Keith served as governor of Pennsylvania from 1717 to 1726; his promise of aid led Franklin to go to Great Britain to buy printing equipment; Franklin soon learned the governor had no money, and Keith later spent time in jail because he couldn't pay his bills

Want to Know More?

More Books to Read

Burgan, Michael. *The Declaration of Independence*. Minneapolis: Compass Point Books, 2001.

Burke, Rick. *Benjamin Franklin*. Chicago: Heinemann Library, 2003.

Donlan, Leni. *Benjamin Franklin: A Life Well Lived*. Chicago: Raintree, 2008.

Gunderston, Jessica. *The Second Continental Congress*. Minneapolis: Compass Point Books, 2008.

Van Vleet, Carmella. *Amazing Ben Franklin Inventions You Can Build Yourself*. White River Junction, Vt.: Nomad Press, 2007.

On the Web

For more information on this topic, use FactHound.

1. Go to *www.facthound.com*

2. Choose your grade level.

3. Begin your search.

This book's ID number is 9780756541194

FactHound will find the best sites for you.

On the Road

Benjamin Franklin National Memorial	**Franklin Court on Market Street**
222 N. 20th St.	314–322 Market St.
Philadelphia, PA	Philadelphia, PA
215/448-1200	215/965-2305
Housed in the Franklin Institute Science Museum, the memorial includes a large marble statue of Franklin and an exhibit hall	Site of a former Franklin home, now home to an underground museum focusing on Franklin's life and times

Look for more We the People Biographies:

Civil War Spy: Elizabeth Van Lew

Confederate Commander: General Robert E. Lee

Confederate General: Stonewall Jackson

First of First Ladies: Martha Washington

A Signer for Independence: John Hancock

Soldier and Founder: Alexander Hamilton

Union General and 18th President: Ulysses S. Grant

A complete list of We the People titles is available on our Web site:
www.compasspointbooks.com

Index

About the Author

Michael Burgan is a freelance writer of books for children and adults. A history graduate of the University of Connecticut, he has written more than 100 fiction and nonfiction children's books. For adult audiences, he has written news articles, essays, and plays. Michael Burgan is a recipient of an Educational Press Association of America award.